The Moon

by Martha E. H. Rustad

Consulting Editor: Gail Saunders-Smith, Ph.D.

Consultant: James Gerard
Aerospace Education Specialist
Kennedy Space Center

Pebble Books

an imprint of Capstone Press
Mankato, Minnesota

Pebble Books are published by Capstone Press
151 Good Counsel Drive, P.O. Box 669, Mankato, Minnesota 56002
http://www.capstone-press.com

1 2 3 4 5 6 07 06 05 04 03 02

Library of Congress Cataloging-in-Publication Data
Rustad, Martha E. H. (Martha Elizabeth Hillman), 1975–
    The moon / by Martha E.H. Rustad.
    p. cm.—(Out in space)
    Includes bibliographical references and index.
    Summary: Photographs and simple text introduce the features of the moon,
Earth's only natural satellite.
    ISBN 0-7368-1177-X
    1. Moon—Juvenile literature. [1. Moon.] I. Title. II. Series.
QB582 .R87 2002
523.3—dc21
                                                                2001004836

Note to Parents and Teachers

The Out in Space series supports national science standards for
units on the universe. This book describes and illustrates the moon.
The photographs support early readers in understanding the text.
This book also introduces early readers to subject-specific
vocabulary words, which are defined in the Words to Know section.
Early readers may need assistance to read some words and to use
the Table of Contents, Words to Know, Read More, Internet Sites,
and Index/Word List sections of the book.

Table of Contents

Look up in the sky.
The moon is high above.

6

The moon is out in space.
It is very far from Earth.

The moon is round
and rocky. The surface
of the moon has craters.

The moon is much
smaller than Earth.
About 50 moons
could fit inside Earth.

The sun shines on the moon. The moon reflects the sun's light to Earth. The moon seems to shine.

13

Earth rotates once each day. The moon looks like it moves from east to west as Earth rotates.

The moon orbits Earth once every 28 days. The same side of the moon always faces Earth.

We sometimes see the moon during the day. We sometimes see the moon at night.

new moon

first quarter

full moon

third quarter

20

The moon seems
to change shape
every night.

Words to Know

crater—a large hole in a surface

Earth—the planet where we live; the moon is about 239,000 miles (385,000 kilometers) from Earth.

orbit—to move around an object in space; the moon orbits Earth in about 28 days.

reflect—to bounce back light; the sun's light reflects off the moon.

rotate—to spin around; Earth rotates once every 24 hours.

sun—a star that gives Earth light and warmth; a star is a large ball of burning gases in space; the sun is about 93 million miles (150 million kilometers) from Earth.

Read More

Branley, Franklyn M. *What the Moon Is Like.* Let's-Read-and-Find-Out Science. New York: HarperCollins, 2000.

Furniss, Tim. *The Moon.* Spinning through Space. Austin, Texas: Raintree Steck-Vaughn, 2001.

Simon, Seymour. *The Moon.* New York: Simon and Schuster Books for Young Readers, 2003.

Internet Sites

BrainPOP: The Moon
http://www.brainpop.com/science/space/moon

NASA Kids: Moon
http://kids.msfc.nasa.gov/Earth/Moon

The Space Place
http://spaceplace.jpl.nasa.gov

Index/Word List

Word Count: 126
Early-Intervention Level: 15

Credits
Timothy Halldin, cover designer and interior illustrator; Kimberly Danger, Mary Englar, and Jo Miller, photo researchers

Gary Milburn/TOM STACK & ASSOCIATES, 12
John Gerlach/TOM STACK & ASSOCIATES, 4
PhotoDisc, Inc., 6, 8, 10, 12 (inset), 14, 16, 20 (all)
Unicorn Stock Photos/Mark Romesser, 1
Visuals Unlimited/Arthur Morris, cover; John Gerlach, 18